COME

HOME

TO

YOURSELF

DÉJÀ RAE

THOUGHT
CATALOG
Books

THOUGHTCATALOG.COM
NEW YORK · LOS ANGELES

THOUGHT CATALOG Books

Published by Thought Catalog Books, an imprint of the digital magazine Thought Catalog, which is owned and operated by The Thought & Expression Company LLC, an independent media organization based in Brooklyn, New York and Los Angeles, California.

This book was produced by Chris Lavergne and Noelle Beams with art direction and design by KJ Parish. Special thanks to Isidoros Karamitopoulos for circulation management.

thoughtcatalog.com | shopcatalog.com

Made in the United States of America.

ISBN 978-1-949759-52-5

I used to dream about the day
you would finally love me.

I crafted storylines and scenarios, I imagined every little detail in my mind, anxiously waiting for the day to come. I thought about the words you would say, the way I would feel, the light in my eyes that would finally resurface after all this time apart. I thought about the way we would laugh together so nostalgically, reflecting back on all our missed time. I thought about the secrets we would share, the love we would make, the life we would create.

But even as I watched the years pass and seasons change, and the leaves fall and blossom over and over again—*you still didn't love me.* My days became longer, the winters felt colder, the dreams I had of us became distant and dismal.

And then on one summer day, I sat down and looked deeply into myself. I felt the sun shining on my skin and the breeze swirling through my hair. I heard birds chirping, and people laughing, and in that very moment I realized it had been years since I had truly felt anything besides the longing for you to love me.

It turns out, in the seasons I spent waiting for you, I was withdrawing from myself. I was so consumed in my dreams, I lost sight of my own life. I had forgotten that the earth was spinning, that time was passing, that there was a world out there waiting for my attention.

I no longer dream about the day you will finally love me, because I have found that love in myself. My dreams no longer consist of you; my power does not lie with someone else.

Table of Contents

Section I

TRUTH

Your capacity to love is marked
by your capacity to be alone.

People can only love you to the extent they love themselves. People can only see you as clearly as they see themselves. People can only understand you to the depth that they understand themselves.

Do not be disheartened by the people who can't love you, who can't see you, who can't understand you.

Their perception of you is merely a reflection of themselves.

Some people *want* love, but don't know *how* to love.

Love is both a feeling and an action. Just because someone *wants* to love you does not mean they know *how* to love you. This disparity often causes us to open our arms to the wrong people. We assume that emotion will evoke action. We think a feeling is enough to fulfill us.

The truth is, there is a learning curve with love. It takes practice, patience, and persistence to learn how to properly love another.

Some will step up to the challenge, others will fall short.

If someone tells you they're emotionally unavailable, please believe them.

You're not going to change their mind. You're not going to shake the ground they walk on and reroute their course. You're just not.

Please understand, if someone is not ready for love, there is nothing you can say and nothing you can do that will make them love you. You will only end up breaking your own heart.

Believe their actions, believe what they tell you.

You deserve to be loved freely.

Not everyone has the capacity for intimacy.

It's not that they don't love you or don't care about your feelings, they just haven't given themselves permission to feel. They haven't allotted themselves the space to care. They've settled on the surface and refuse to go any deeper.

Intimacy requires vulnerability, it requires us to open the door to our caged hearts and expose our most tender spaces.

But many people have decided the possibility of pain overrides the ecstasy of love.

Sometimes people just want the easier choice.

Sometimes people aren't ready for someone who will challenge them. They don't want someone who will mirror back their insecurities, who will push them to grow outside themselves. They aren't willing to share such a depth of love, they aren't prepared for the pain that may come with it.

So, they opt for the easier choice.
They choose complacency, they settle in the safety zone.

But at a great cost.

Many people never leave the safety zone.
Many people never experience what true love really is.

Do not stay in spaces that are not conducive to your growth.

Do not shrink your capacity to love for those that do not have the capacity to love you.

Do not compromise your standards of connection only to grasp at scraps of affection.

Never again will you convince others of your worth.
Never again will you betray yourself.

Never again will you beg for love.

Pay close attention to the way people show up in the details.

How do they react when something bad happens? How do they behave when something good happens? How do they treat their friends, their family, their service workers, their community members, their pets? How do they act toward the people that test their patience? How do they interact through moments of inconvenience and disagreement? How do they speak to themselves through seasons of failure and setback?

The thing is, anyone can do the grand gestures. It's not as hard as you think. We grow up watching romance films and listening to love songs, and through that, we subconsciously learn all the right things to say and do to make someone fall in love with you.

But the details aren't so easily framed; they can only be forged to such an extent. The details reflect their character, the details highlight the things that really matter, the things that really define who someone is. The details are who you will marry, who will raise your kids, who will support you throughout your life.

So please, pay close attention to the details, because the details define the truth.

Please don't wait around any longer for someone to fall in love with you.

Maybe they will eventually love you, or maybe they won't. That's not the point. The point is that when you wait for someone to decide whether you are worthy of their love— you hold space in your life for indecision. And that uncertainty will soon bleed into every part of your life.

You'll allow yourself to stay at a job that doesn't value your skills. You'll linger in environments that are not conducive to your growth. You'll continue to attract people and experiences that stir up uneasiness and doubt.

Because *every* decision we make impacts *every* part of our life.

If we decide we deserve more in one area, we will receive more in all areas. If we decide we will settle in one situation, we will settle in all situations.

Waiting around for someone to love you is more than just one decision.

It creates the foundation for the type of life you are willing to accept.

Do you really want to be with someone who makes you question your self-worth?

Do you really want to spend your time worrying about whether you are loved?

Do you really want a love like that?

Do you really want a life like that?

Sometimes we stay in relationships not because we desire our partner, but rather, we desire a connection. We crave love, we want intimacy, yet we don't want the person we're receiving it from. We conflate attachment with affection, we trade authenticity for availability. We betray the voice inside of us that whispers melodies of truth. We abandon our deepest desires; we're willing to sacrifice our true potential for love.

But the longer we lie to ourselves, the deeper our truth will sink, and the heavier it will become. We cannot hide from the reality that lingers inside. Every time they disappoint us, every time an argument passes without closure, and every time a milestone goes unacknowledged, the whispers of truth will come crawling back, gently nudging us towards the light we're hiding from.

Are you holding on to someone
who is letting go of you?

Are you clinging on to something
that is releasing its grip on you?

It is a difficult reality to know the truth yet lack the strength to make the right decision.

You can be fully aware that an environment is not good for you, yet willingly choose to stay there. You can consciously know what's best for you, while continually deciding to ignore that truth. You can have a great capacity to understand, you can know exactly why you act the way you act, why you do the things you do. You can have all the answers, know the right resolutions, yet perpetually choose pain over an actual solution.

My friend, you are not alone. It is a trying task to honor what you feel.

Do not judge yourself, do not hold resentment for taking the wrong path.

This is what life is all about. The wrong decisions will eventually lead you to the right ones. But you will never facilitate self-growth through negative self-talk. You will never make the right decisions by blaming yourself for the wrong ones. You will never achieve transformation through condemnation.

Be easy on yourself.
Have compassion for your flaws.
Breathe in and breathe out.

You are doing just fine.

There is a fundamental difference between needing someone and wanting someone.

When you feel as though you need someone, it's often because there is something empty inside of yourself. That emptiness causes you to look outward, in an attempt to ease the loneliness. And when you do finally find a crutch, you will wring out every drop of their love to fill that empty space. Your connection will inherently be centered around you, it will be centered around receiving.

But when you want someone, your connection will be centered around them, it will be centered around giving. You will choose this person because you genuinely admire them. You will love them for who they are, rather than for how they can make you feel. You will focus on pouring your energy into them, you will figure out ways to make their days easier, to make their life more meaningful.

That is why relationships that are based on need often don't work. Because if one person needs the other, the love is only flowing from one direction, and if both people need each other, *the love isn't flowing at all.*

When you bounce from relationship to relationship, when you sweep through person to person, you will often lose the concept of who you really are and what you really love. You will blindly weave through life, allowing others to mold you along the way. You will shapeshift into different versions of yourself, just so you can feel wanted in that season of time. You will forget about your passions; you will leave your desires to decay in the dark. You will completely lose sight of who you are because you no longer care about what you love—you only care about who's going to love you.

But once you finally let go and surrender to the depths of loneliness, you will discover what's been lingering inside of you. You will begin to see who you *truly* are—who you've *always* been. Life will become boundless and vibrant; you will start unpacking your desires and dreams.

And you will begin to understand that the love you craved was never in the hands of another human—it was always inside of you, patiently waiting for you to come home.

Are you yourself?

Or are you a collection of
pieces from other people?

Stop putting your energy where it is not appreciated nor reciprocated.

Stop preemptively plotting every move you make and every word you say.

If you find that you are constantly calculating your communication, thus complicating your connection, you should reconsider the type of love you want.

Love should not feel calculated or complicated.

And if you continue to participate in this type of love, you must take responsibility for perpetuating the problem.

My love, good things don't always last forever.
And that's okay. They're not supposed to.

More and more good things are flowing your way.
More people, more love, more experiences, more
opportunities.

But if you keep holding on to the past, you will not
have space for your future.

Sometimes beautiful people come into your life for only a season of time simply to show you that good people exist.

They come to remind you that love is worth fighting for, that there are people in this world who will see you for who you truly are. They come to teach you how to love yourself, to nudge you in the right direction.

And oftentimes, these people leave just as quickly as they came.

Let them go with love. They were never yours to keep.

You are afraid to leave because you are afraid to be alone.
You're afraid to open the door and see what lurks on the
other side. You're afraid to finally face the truth you've been
hiding from and you're afraid of the grief that's to come.

But friend, you are not alone in your loneliness.
You will not be forsaken in your fears.

There is a strength inside of you that will guide you.
There is a power within you waiting to appear.

Remember,

It is better to be lonely by yourself
than lonely beside someone else.

You don't need a savior.
You don't need an emotional crutch.
You don't need someone to distract you from your pain any longer.

You are capable of healing yourself, of freeing yourself, of expanding yourself into the person you're meant to be.

You don't need a savior.

No matter what you do, you're always making a commitment.

Some people commit themselves to love; others commit to pain.

Some people commit to expansion; others commit to stagnation.

We must be cognizant of the language we use.

It's easy to slip into seasons of suffering when your personal narrative paints you as the victim. It's easy to make a shelter in your sadness when you've deemed yourself as powerless.

But what if instead, every time you've expended your energy, you reminded yourself that you are making a commitment.

I am pledging allegiance to my anguish.
I am devoting myself to my destruction.

It doesn't sound so appealing anymore, does it?

Stop making excuses. Stop settling for what's in front of you. Stop pretending that this life is what you want, that this person is who you need, that your desires are out of reach.

Every night when you go to sleep and sink into yourself— you know what is right. You know what your heart wants. You cannot hide from the tenacity of your truth. Sure, you can try to justify their inconsistencies and defend their deficiencies, but that inner voice, that inner knowing will never subside until you concede. It will never stop whispering until you decide to listen.

Stop lying to yourself.

Your energy is your most
expensive currency.

And not everyone can afford it.

If you don't want to play games, then stop playing into them.

It's really that simple.

When you stop entertaining half-loves, inconsistencies, and minimum efforts, you naturally weed out everything and everyone that is not aligned with the level of love you desire.

But if you continue to succumb to what you're trying to over-come, your relationship patterns will never come undone.

It's only a matter of time.

You can leave now. But if not now, you can leave in a few months. And if not then, maybe you will leave in a year, or two years, or ten years—*it doesn't really matter.*

The point is—whatever is not meant for you will never be yours.

So, it's for you to decide how much time you want to spend holding on to something that does not belong to you.

When we cling onto things that feel good, it's often because we fear that something so good won't come around again. We fear that this person, this experience, this feeling, if it goes away, nothing of that magnitude will ever happen again.

But that's just not true. Good things are abundant. Good feelings are abundant. Happiness is infinite, the beauty of this world is boundless and endless.

The moment you begin to perceive everything good in life as perpetual, the less fearful you are of letting go of the things that are no longer serving you.

No matter how far you are, no matter how much time has gone by, and no matter how much distance is in between, they can surely feel your love.

Love is boundless and abundant—there is no barrier that can restrict the flow of love from one human to another.

Rest assured that your love is never put to waste.

To truly let go of the past, you must take responsibility for the part you played.

If you only place blame on the other person, while victimizing yourself, you will stay stagnant, shackled to your suffering. You will continue to reside in your resentment; you'll make a home inside your heartache.

But when you reflect with gentle honesty and take accountability for the role you may have played, you set yourself free. You detach yourself from the past and gravitate toward higher frequencies.

We are constantly co-creating with one another.
There's always a lesson to be learned.

Things usually happen the way they're supposed to.

Oftentimes, rejection is redirection, closed doors are protecting you from what's lurking around the corner. Plans fall through because better things are coming in. The wrong people pass by because the right ones are moving closer.

Adopting this mindset will set you free. It will liberate you from living in the past and rescue you from ruminating over all the things that didn't happen the way you hoped they would.

Remember my friend; things usually happen *exactly* the way they're supposed to.

If you decide they're not the
one for you—*congratulations.*

You're now one step closer
to finding your person.

There is an abundance of love in this world.
There is an abundance of relationships, experiences and connections.

If this one didn't work out for you, there is surely an overflow of more waiting for you. It's easy to sink into sentiment that this is the end, this person is the end, that life will not go on without them. You convince yourself that you'll never meet someone with the same chemistry, you'll never find such a magnetic connection.

But my friend, that's just not true. You have been loved, you have lost love, and you will find love again. Letting go of lost love is the most expansive thing you can do for yourself, because through this, you tell the universe that you believe in the abundance of love. And even though things didn't work out this time, you believe that new and beautiful things are on their way.

Remind yourself, there is an abundance of love in this world.

Remember—not only are you learning lessons from the people you experience, but the people you experience are learning lessons through you.

The universe uses relationships to heal us, to teach us, to grow us into who we're destined to be.

The seeds you plant will *always* become fruitful with time.

Do not let pride get in the way of love.

Too much pride will cause you to walk away from genuine connections because you don't want to appear weak. Too much pride will lead you to devalue others because you can't admit when you are wrong.

Too much pride will leave you lonely.
It will lead you astray.

It will cause you to lose the people that love you most.

If you don't know how someone feels about you—*just ask.*

Stop exhausting yourself playing the guessing game. Stop over-analyzing every behavior and every conversation, trying to make sense of the situation. Just ask.

Communication is the most powerful tool in our toolbox, yet it often goes unused, out of fear of what it might lead to. Many of us would rather play the guessing game because uncertainty feels better than rejection. Sure, we may not know how they really feel, but at least we don't have to face the possibility of abandonment, we don't have to know the ugly truth, we don't have to make any hard decisions. But the thing about uncertainty is that it keeps us trapped, trapped between what we don't know and what we fear most. And the very walls that keep us cornered also keep us closed-hearted, empty, unfulfilled, and unable to receive true love and intimacy.

Communication sets us free. But communication may also lead us down a path where we're faced with the things that frighten us. Yes, we may get rejected. Yes, we may have to walk away from a situation that we've previously found comfort in. Yes, we may have to confront our trauma and heal our deepest wounds.

But at least we are free.

Free to move forward, free to make decisions, free to live our lives without the constant grief of not knowing whether we are loved.

It is better to feel pain from the truth than to be fooled by a lie.

Don't ever be embarrassed about the love you give.

Don't ever be ashamed of saying too much, for feeling too deeply, for being the one that cares more.

There is no braver endeavor than giving affection.
There is no stronger pursuit than showing passion.

Your vulnerability will
always be rewarded.

When you cast loving thoughts toward others, you heal yourself, and in turn, heal the world.

Loving thoughts have the capacity to completely change our perception. Loving thoughts have the power to slow down our heart rate, comfort our mind, ease our suffering. Loving thoughts can cure sickness, heal pain, and transform the world.

When a situation arises that frustrates you, cast out a loving thought. Remind yourself of the good in every circumstance. Stand strong in divine truth.

You will soon begin to see that all your problems no longer feel painful, all your annoyances no longer fight for your attention.

The energy you surround yourself with, the people you allow access to you, and the environments that you linger in will indefinitely determine the way you experience and perceive life.

It is your responsibility to constantly evaluate whether your surroundings are inspiring you to become a better person or requiring you to dim your light.

Stop people-pleasing.

Stop saying yes when you want to say no. Stop pursuing avenues that aren't in alignment with your values. Stop running after unrequited love. Stop shrinking yourself, stop belittling your worth, stop compromising your needs.

My friend, don't you see?

When you give without regard for yourself, you continue to attract people who only want to take from you.

Someone's acceptance or rejection of you should never dictate how you feel about yourself.

If you don't want to casually date someone, stop settling for casual dating.

Stop compromising your needs, your values, and your desires, simply because you want to be loved. If pretending like you don't like someone is the only way to attract that person, that's probably not a person you want to be with in the first place. If you must quiet your voice and shrink your needs to mold into the type of person that your partner desires, then that was never your person to begin with. If you feel the need to calculate every conversation, time out every text message, and plan out every exchange, then that's probably not your person. If being real with someone pushes them away, that's not a person you want to be with.

As a collective, we must stop compromising our desire for true intimacy.

From the moment we enter this world, love and connection is what guides us through. We would have not been able to survive without it, and this truth does not change with time. Do not concede to the culture. Do not allow society to sculpt you. You don't need to be cold to be loved. You don't need to be ambivalent to be desired.

You can, and you will, find someone who wants to cater to all your needs.

Not expressing how you truly feel
for the purpose of maintaining
peace is an act of self-betrayal.

Self-care doesn't always look like shopping splurges, fancy dinners, and spa treatments.

Oftentimes, self-care doesn't look so pretty, it doesn't feel so easy.

It looks like 6am workouts and home cooked meals. It feels like vulnerability and discomfort. It's nights at home and Sundays spent deep-cleaning. Self-care is organizing, planning, preparing, and crossing off to-do lists. It's making your bed in the morning and watering your plants when they need love. It's giving away old clothes and calling your grandparents to check in. Self-care is setting boundaries, facing challenges, and standing in your truth, even when it hurts the most.

Self-care is self-discipline.

And self-discipline gives us the confidence to care for ourselves even more.

The way you allow others to treat you is a reflection of your perceived self-worth.

If reading that sentence causes you discomfort—my friend, it's okay. The beautiful thing about self-worth is that you can always build more of it. The way you view yourself, the way you treat yourself, and the situations that surround you can be changed at any moment. You don't have to keep settling for less, you don't need to keep compromising your desires.

All you must do is decide. Decide that you want more for your life. Decide that you will no longer tolerate people and situations that don't serve you. And start building your life on that foundation. Create experiences that honor those principles and don't waver in what you stand for.

Make a vow to yourself today that you will never again betray who you are, what you value, and what you want for your life.

Allow people to be who they truly are and let them show up in the way they naturally do.

And then decide if that is enough for you.

Section II

PAIN

Everything shines before you're ready to leave.

In the days leading up to your departure, your circum-
stances may suddenly improve, people will put their best
foot forward, your life will unexpectedly feel aligned.

Do not be fooled, for it is only smoke and mirrors.

The truth will always glisten through the gimmicks.

When you finally decide to jump—you will hit the ground hard. Your entire foundation will shake, everything you thought you knew about yourself will be questioned. You will wonder whether you made the right decision, and you will consider going back. You will think of all the reasons why you can't move forward, and you will focus on everything that you lack.

But friend—if you are hurting, you are healing.
You are breaking through your bondage.

There is an abundance of beauty that awaits you, please remember, this universe will never forsake you.

You don't need to get rid
of your loneliness.

You need to get comfortable in it.

Instead of running away from your pain, why don't you try running towards it?

Why don't you try embracing it? Why don't you soak in it and sit through it? What would happen if you gave it permission to take over? What kind of realizations could you have, what kind of transformation would you go through?

The more you practice feeling your pain, the less scared you are to confront it the next time it comes knocking at your door.

You're never going to escape it.

So why don't you just face it?

It's going to take time.

It's going to take time to let go and move on. Grant yourself graduality. Have patience with the process. There is no rush, there is no final destination.

When you try to expedite your pain, you inadvertently prolong it. You breeze through the lessons and skip over the revelations. In doing this, you deprive yourself of the opportunity to reroute, and thus, you continue on the same cycle. The pain eventually comes back, darker and heavier than before.

My friend, it's going to take time, and it's going to be very difficult at first. But eventually, you will reach a point where each day gets a little easier, each morning becomes a bit brighter. And you will look back on your journey with reverence. You will have a deep appreciation for the process, a full understanding of why healing had to happen unhurriedly.

The ultimate test is to sit back when you want to move forward.

To stay quiet when every inch of you wants to reach out.

To trust in the process instead of trying to figure out the future.

The hardest part of letting go is having to celebrate their success from the sidelines.

I know you want to be there to congratulate them, I know you want to tell them how proud you are of their progress.

But sometimes, we must celebrate in silence.
We must appreciate their existence from a distance.

And even if all you ever have is a view from the sidelines, you can be sure that your support will always be sensed.

To love someone is both the greatest
feat and the most painful lesson.

The first step in healing is hurting.

You must bring everything to the surface. Every situation that has scarred you, every person that has betrayed you, every goodbye that has left you broken. You must confront it head-on. You must welcome it into your space.

And it's going to sting deeply.

But friend—if you are hurting, you are healing.
You are well on your way to brighter seasons.

I pray this heartbreak leads you to
fall deeper in love with yourself.

Feel your feelings subjectively, then reflect on them objectively.

Feel the pain, soak in the sorrow. Cry it out, write it out, hold space for your heartache. Take a break from work, watch your favorite movies, order your favorite food. Indulge in your disappointment.

But after you've felt your pain, you must think about it.

Consider why you're feeling this way. What part of you feels triggered? Is this something new or something old? Is there a pattern that is repeating? Is there a change that needs to be made?

What can you take accountability for? What can you learn from this? How can you grow from this?

If you only feel your feelings, you deprive yourself of the opportunity to understand.

If you only think about your feelings, you deprive yourself of the opportunity to expand.

In order to move past it, you must first walk through it.

You will never fully let go of a past situation, a previous experience, or a former lover, if you continually hide from the pain associated with that time, that incident, that person.

You must bring it all to the surface.
You must feel your pain, deeply and woefully.

And after you do, not only will you have found a bigger and brighter version of yourself, but you will no longer be fearful of the pain that lurks in the corner of every life experience.

You will no longer be afraid to feel.
You will no longer be afraid to live.
You will no longer be afraid to be human.

Your emotions are just visitors, and you must treat them as such.

Welcome them into your space; invite them into your home. Give them your undivided attention, as they've only come for a short period. Cater to them, inquire about their origins.

Their presence may briefly disrupt your routine.
You will need to create space for their visit.

But once their stay has ended and a new day dawns, your feelings will kindly depart. You must kiss them goodbye and let them go, for they were never yours to keep.

You can have a deep appreciation for life and a full awareness of your favor yet still feel sad about your circumstances.

You don't need to compartmentalize your emotions. Gratitude and grief are not mutually exclusive.

You can feel joy and sorrow at the same time.
You can feel fear and faith at the same time.
You are entitled to your pain.

Please give yourself permission to feel.

The hard things lead to the good things.

The seasons that test your strength, the situations that feel uncomfortable, and the decisions that require courage, are the very things that will lead you toward true fulfillment.

If you're willing to walk through the fire and surrender to uncertainty, you will eventually experience all the beauty that awaits you on the other side.

So stop running away from the hard things.

Because the hard things build the foundation for the good things to grow.

As you become clear on the type of people you want in your life, you will often find loneliness before you find love. You will be called to sit in solitude before you meet the people that can reach you at your level.

This happens for two reasons.

One, by standing strong in your truth, you naturally weed out everyone and everything that doesn't align with you. People and spaces you once associated with will dwindle away with time.

Two, you will continually be tested with situations that push past your boundaries, that compromise your standards. It is your responsibility to protect your peace, even when the loneliness is sinking inside of you.

You must keep an enduring faith that this universe hears you and will see you through to the end.

When you uphold your boundaries, some people will try to make you doubt yourself. They will call you sensitive, they will claim you're overreacting. They will say it's not that serious.

That is because people who don't have boundaries lack the capacity to understand yours.

You don't need to explain yourself.
You don't need to defend your principles.

Simply allow your light to illuminate the dark.

People from your past will slither back into your life not because they still want you, but rather, to see if you still want them.

Please do not fall for their deception.
Do not allow them access to you.

Do not jeopardize your growth for their gain.

When the same relationship patterns appear, this is the universe communicating with you. There may be something you need to change, there may be a lesson that needs to be learned, or there may be a temptation that you must overcome.

Instead of blaming yourself for falling into the same cycle, praise yourself for creating the opportunity to overcome.

Take a step back and look at the situation objectively. What patterns do you see? What triggers are appearing? Have you seen this before, have you felt this before? What decision did you make last time? What could you do differently this time?

Friend, this is an opportunity for you to learn, to grow, to transcend the season you've been stuck in. Don't be so hard on yourself. This is beautiful. This is the process.

This is you turning into the person you're destined to be.

There is no such thing as failing a test.

You are simply revising a lesson.

You're going to make mistakes.

Sometimes you're going to get it wrong. Sometimes you'll have to relearn a lesson. Sometimes you're going to fall, you're going to choose the wrong choice, you're going to look back and wish you would have done things differently.

My friend, it's okay. You are human. You are allowed to make mistakes. You don't need to get it right all the time. You don't need to have all the right answers and make all the right decisions.

But when you do fall back, you must love yourself through that. You must be willing to forgive yourself indefinitely. You must offer yourself compassion through every setback.

You will never achieve growth through guilt.
You will never achieve breakthrough by bondage.

When you feel anxious, ground yourself in truth.

It's okay to be scared, it's normal to feel nervous. These are human emotions. They are not to be feared, they are to be felt.

But if we choose to ignore our feelings, to pretend that this life does not phase us, we will fuel fire to the fear inside of us. This fear will bleed into our relationships, it will fester in our thoughts, it will mold itself into our character.

Your emotions need a release.

Feel them deeply. Don't judge yourself, don't compare your growth to others. You are valid. Your emotions are valid. You are allowed to express your pain.

Remind yourself of this, repeatedly. As many times as it takes.

Ground yourself so deeply in truth that nothing in this world can shake your foundation.

Try reframing the way you think.

Instead of thinking,
Does he like me?

Think,
Do I like him?

Instead of thinking,
I'm scared of what's going to happen.

Think,
I'm excited to see what God has in store for me.

Instead of thinking,
I'm worried about the future.

Think,
I'm grateful for what's to come.

Oftentimes you can't change the situation, but
you can certainly change the way you think.

Do not measure the amount of love in your life by whether you have a romantic partner.

Love is everywhere and all around you. You can tap into it at any moment.

You can create it within yourself or destroy it by fixating on someone else.

Your life is what you choose to see.

If you choose to take note of everything you lack, to count all the ways life has gone wrong, to focus on all the people that don't love you—your life will surely feel empty.

But if you choose to count your blessings, to find joy in the small things, to commit yourself to love and gratitude—your life will feel full.

If someone were to wave a magic wand and tell you with absolute certainty you would meet your soulmate one year from now, how would you feel? What kind of decisions would you make? What type of experiences would you chase after? Would you worry so much about the details? Would you spend so much time focusing on who isn't paying attention to you?

My friend, this is the way you must live your life, with absolute certainty that there is a person in this world for you. Even when there is no evidence, nothing to show for it, you must believe it to your core.

This undying faith will not only attract the right person, but it will set you free and allow you to fully enjoy your existence.

Life becomes easier when you stop taking things so personally.

Stop overthinking everything. Stop trying to figure out why they didn't respond, or why they don't love you, or why you've been alone for so long. You will exhaust yourself trying to find answers that you may simply never know.

Let it go, friend. Let it all go. Let it roll off you like a beautiful summer day. Let life flow through you. Let experiences flow to you. Allow people to gently pass in and out of your life.

Life is far too short to take everything so personally.

Sometimes it's just not worth your energy.

It's not worth your time to sit there and explain.
You don't always need to prove your point.
You don't always have to say your piece.

Sometimes silence is the strongest solution.

A victim mentality blocks your blessings.

When you believe that life is working against you, you will subconsciously seek out situations that reinforce that reality. You will only pay attention to the people that are not paying attention to you. You will double down on your downfall; you will create a life that corroborates your personal narrative.

When you step out of a victim mentality, and step into your agency, you will see all the ways life is working for you. You will recognize your favor; you will have gratitude for your journey.

Most importantly, you will attract abundance.
Your life will become a beautiful reflection of everything you desire.

You must actively choose healing over suffering.

Pain is inevitable, but suffering is a choice.

Please stop criticizing yourself.

Stop nitpicking everything you do, everything you say. Stop judging the way you show up in this world. Stop entertaining the thoughts that tell you life would be better if you looked like this, or sounded like that, or had this much money, or that much success. Stop it.

My friend, the way you speak to yourself is not dependent on your circumstances. Even when you find the relationship, when you get the job, when you receive the recognition, you will continue to criticize yourself.

Our self-talk is not contingent upon our external world but is a reflection of our internal beliefs.

Do not give power to your anxious thoughts.

Throughout life, anxious thoughts will inevitably appear. They will often come in seasons of setback, and they will fight for your attention. Do not fall for their deception, do not walk in their direction. You must perceive them from a distance and meet them with resistance.

The thoughts you give power to will flourish. They will continue to reappear, stronger and more persuasive each time around. They will sink deeper, they will feel heavier, they will slowly latch onto your light.

You must repeatedly put them down and ground yourself in truth.

Your thoughts are like seeds, and the ones you water will grow roots in your beliefs.

Make it a priority to check in with your higher self every day.

When life gets busy, our minds get busy as well. If we don't intentionally take moments to slow down and realign ourselves, we will eventually feel consumed by chaos. Bouts of irritability will start to creep up; we'll suddenly feel short-tempered and impatient. We'll start looking for the bad in everything, we'll only focus on the negative qualities in the people that surround us.

You must repeatedly realign yourself; you must consciously remind yourself of the truth. Wake up a bit earlier every morning and write down your frustrations. Meditate through it, pray on it, cry about it. Ask God to guide you, ask the universe to remind you of truth.

You will soon find that all the little things that once frustrated you no longer grab your attention.

Stop thinking about him.
Stop watching the clock. Stop checking your phone. Stop fantasizing about what's going to happen or what's not going to happen or when it's going to happen or if it's going to happen.

Stop wasting moments of your life waiting around for someone else to show up. Don't you see? Time is passing and the world is moving with or without you.

Do you really want to spend your time waiting on someone else?

Do you really want to spend your life existing for someone else?

Release your worries and go live your life.
There is a world out there waiting for your attention.

The amount of energy you give to your circumstances is indicative of the power your circumstances have over you.

If you keep talking about a situation, if you keep consulting others for advice, and if you keep spending your energy trying to find answers—*you are never going to move forward.*

Growth comes from letting go.

Healing comes from acceptance.

Prioritize your peace.

Stop giving your energy to
people that exhaust you.

Stop putting yourself in situations
that compromise your well-being.

Stop opening doors to spaces
that restrict your abundance.

Stop betraying yourself for
the satisfaction of others.

The reason you are so focused on finding a relationship is because deep down you fear it may never happen. A part of you believes it's not possible. A piece of you thinks you will always be stuck in a cycle of failed relationships.

My friend, the first step in enjoying your singleness is fixing your beliefs.

Because if you truly, deeply, with an unwavering faith, believed you would eventually find your person, you wouldn't worry so much about the details of when, why, and how.

Instead, you would focus on enjoying your season of singleness because you understand it's not going to last forever.

If you don't genuinely believe your dream person exists—you will always end up settling for less.

You will repeatedly look past red flags and excuse minimum efforts because you don't think the whole package is possible. You will settle for mediocrity, for good enough, for half-love.

And in doing this, you betray yourself.
You sacrifice your greatest potential for true connection.

Think about it. Someone else in this world has an idea of their dream person. They've crafted a list of all their characteristics; they've held a firm vision of what their union will someday look like. They are certain about this person, utterly convinced that they will one day cross paths. And that person is you.

You are someone else's dream person.

So, if you exist—*why wouldn't they exist too?*

Don't worry so much about love.

Don't worry so much about who's going to love you, or how they're going to love you, or when you're going to find love.

Love is the most infinite and effortless presence in this world. It's found in the tiny crevices of human nature—in the way flowers bloom and in the way birds always have enough food to eat. It's found in hospital rooms, and grocery stores, in home cooked meals, and in the smiles of passing strangers. Love is in the music you listen to, and in the jokes you make, and it's in the way you always return home for the holidays. Love is 'are you okay,' and 'get home safe,' and 'did you have enough food to eat.' Love is the way your heart beats every day and how your body wakes up every morning and how your soul continues to exist so freely.

You don't need to worry about love. It is all around you, every day, in every moment. It can reach you at your best and it will meet you at your worst. There is no force in this world stronger than love.

There is no reason to believe that love cannot find you.

If you want to be truly happy, you must commit yourself to something bigger than finding a relationship.

If finding a partner, or being with your partner, is the center of your life—you will always feel dissatisfied.

When you are fully consumed in another, you give up your own energy, your own agency, as a distinct individual in this world. You put all your power into the hands of another human.

My friend, you were put in this world for a divine purpose.

Go figure out what that purpose is.

Society has told us the ultimate goal of life is to find a partner, get married, and start a family. While these are beautiful milestones, if our only objective in life is centered around another person—we will always be left unfulfilled.

Every day that passes that we haven't found our person, we will experience it as though it were a day wasted. Every holiday we spend alone, we will feel our dream dwindling away. Every morning we wake up and reach for the empty space beside us, we will fear our life may never reach its full potential.

My dear friend, your ultimate goal in life should be to simply enjoy your existence. To pursue the things that make you happy. To discover your truest self and love her through and through. To honor who you are, and from that place of authenticity, create the most beautiful things. To develop an unwavering love for your life, and through that, plant seeds of inspiration in all the people you encounter.

That is your legacy. There is not a person that can take that away from you.

Your destiny, your impact, your purpose—will never be dependent upon another person.

This is *your* life. *You* are in control. It is time to claim *your* power.

We often think we know what makes us happy, but really, we are projecting the societal scripts of what we're told happiness looks like.

We often think the career, the relationship, the recognition, will finally give us the happiness we're hoping for. We spend hours getting ready to go out at night, when really, our soul wants to stay in. We spend money on material things in an attempt to impress other people, when really, no one notices. We take up so much time seeking success, working toward rewards, looking for validation, only to find the emptiness is still there.

My friend, your happiness must come from within. There is not a person, not an experience, not an opportunity in this world, that will ever give you the joy that you can simply give to yourself.

When you finally decide to choose yourself, you will feel the deepest sense of satisfaction, the most lucid inner knowing that you've chosen the right path.

Despite the discomfort, you will be certain that you've made the right decision.

And as you continue to flow through life, you will repeatedly thank your former self for honoring your future self.

Instead of fixating on what you want to happen, be excited for what God is going to reveal to you.

Everything that happens to you, the good stuff, the bad stuff, the monotonous stuff that gets you from day to day, God uses to mold you into the person you're meant to become.

If someone walks out of your life, rather than clinging on, let go and ask God to show you the lesson in this departure. If you don't get the opportunity you've been praying for, rather than sulking in disappointment, let go and ask God what's coming next.

Everything that happens to you is there to help you in some way, all you must do is open your eyes to it.

Be aware of it.
Be cognizant of the blessings in all things.

You must trust that everything works for the greater good.

Sometimes you get rejected, because someone else is waiting for you. Sometimes your plans fall through, because the universe has bigger plans on the horizon. Sometimes you don't get the opportunity, because someone else needed it more in that moment.

Only God knows the intricacies of all things.

Move forward with loving faith that you are always being guided for the greater good.

Sometimes things from your perspective just don't make sense.

And sometimes they never will.

But maybe things don't always need to make sense, maybe closure doesn't need to be found in every situation.

Maybe the point of all the pain is to strengthen your trust muscle, to develop an unwavering faith in the unknown. To know that through life's most trying circumstances, there is something bigger, something all-knowing, to grasp onto.

Please remember, there is divine order in all things.

And even when things don't make sense to you, that doesn't mean there is no sense in it at all.

Learn how to love in the absence of it.

Learn how to forgive when you don't get an apology.

Learn how to speak highly of those who wronged you.

When you operate from a place of unconditional love, you become a source of light, a source of life, that no person, no situation, and no circumstance can suppress.

When you are no longer afraid of being alone, a different kind of power is unleashed within you.

You will no longer tolerate disrespect; you will not stay in spaces that hinder your growth. You will not settle for people and places that are not in alignment with what you want.

And when you stop doing these things, you generate energy to do so much more. You cultivate the capacity to create, to build, to inspire, to impact. Your life is no longer centered around getting a fix, but is focused on finding fulfillment. Your goals are no longer dependent on someone else, but revolve around yourself.

Your dreams are no longer about finding the missing piece, but rather, maintaining your inner peace.

Section III

ABUNDANCE

The more you focus on finding your purpose, the less you will fixate on finding a relationship.

Your thoughts and actions are often defined by what you consume.

Put down the how-to relationship book for a few days. You don't need to figure anything out. Stop talking to your friends about it. Everything has already been said. Quit fantasizing about a future with that person. They're in the past for a reason.

Shift your focus inward. Consume your mind with things that inspire you. Do something you love. Start that project. Make that phone call. Collaborate with your friends. Pour your energy into the things that give you energy back.

And one day, while you're sipping your morning coffee and writing down your intentions, you will realize it has been weeks since that person crossed your mind. The very person you once thought you couldn't go a day without.

Keep your mind busy and your heart full.

Commit yourself to something, anything.

Commit yourself so wholeheartedly and give nothing the power to stand in the way of you and what you want.

Apathy is the gateway to emptiness. If you have no regard for your life, no interest in pursuing your passions, no concern about the well-being of others, you will perpetually feel unfulfilled.

We were born to care, to connect, to create. We were born with talents that need to be seen, art that needs to be shared, opinions that need to be heard. But if we surrender to apathy, we empty ourselves of all the things that fulfill us, all the things that make us human.

Friend, it doesn't matter how small or how big it is. Commit yourself to it. Even if that looks like finishing a new book, learning a new recipe, or working on a new art project— commit yourself to it. Nurture it, take care of it, hold on to it so delicately as if it were your last will to live. Once you start committing to the small things, you will find yourself caring more about the big things.

It's a process my dear friend, you've got this.

What gives you peace? What makes you feel safe? What feels good? What gives you chills? What inspires you to become a better person? What makes you feel alive? What makes you smile? What makes you forget about the outside world? What centers you? What aligns you? What do you love right now? What did you love when you were young? What are your talents? What are your skills? What do you get complimented on? What do people recognize you for? What is important to you? What do you value? What gives you purpose? What excites you? What do you see in your future? What is your most uninhibited dream?

What are you thinking about right now?

Pursue that.

You know what you truly desire.

When you quiet the noise and ignore the fears, you know the truth. When you sink deep into yourself, you can feel what your heart is longing for.

All the answers you need are inside of you. They are simply waiting for your attention. You don't need to consult every friend, you don't need advice from every book.

All you need to do is sink deeply into yourself and listen to the pulse of your heart. Focus on that inner knowing.

It will guide you to where you're supposed to be.

Many people know what they want but just don't know if it's possible. They don't believe in their ability to get there. They doubt their talents, they question their capabilities. They compare their end goal to their current circumstances and become discouraged by the disparity.

Please remind yourself—good things take time to manifest. Dreams are not achieved all at once. You must gradually build the foundation for your future.

Pay no mind to your uncertainty.

Your desires are there for a reason.

The most enduring happiness comes from being yourself.

It comes from working towards the things you love, expressing the ways you truly feel, sharing the things you want others to see.

I understand the possibility of judgment and criticism is daunting. But friend, no matter what you do in life, people are going to have an opinion on it. People are going to perceive you, critique you, and disagree with you. And there's absolutely nothing wrong with that.

You don't need to be admired by everyone. You don't need everyone to agree with you. The moment you accept this, you free yourself to blossom fully into your truest being. It is better to be judged for who you are than to linger inside a body that doesn't feel like yours.

So please—post that video, start that project, share that artwork, *live your truth*.

The most precious gift you can give yourself comes from honoring your most authentic self.

You can be it all.

You can be introverted and extroverted, you can be reserved and outgoing. You can be open and private, you can be sensitive and unsusceptible. You can be creative and analytical. You can be feminine and you can be masculine. You can love luxury and sustainability. You can be an artist and an analyst. You can love God and you can love science. You can be spiritually aligned while also enjoying the human experience.

My friend, you can be it all. You don't need to pick one. You don't need to build your identity around a single trait or single truth.

From when we are young, the world teaches us that we must tick one box, we must fit into one category, subscribe to one religion, pursue one career. That's because society's objective has always been to limit us, to trap us into a restricted mindset. To make us think there's only one type of beauty, there's only one form of success.

My friend, you were made from an explosion of the universe, hand-crafted by God Herself. You have a direct connection to the creator of existence. You are everything that He is, everything this universe has crafted.

You can be anything you want to be, you can be everything you want to be.

You can be it all.

People love you.

People want to be around you. People see your light and are inspired by it. When you leave the room, they talk about how lovely you are. Strangers notice your beauty; they feel attracted to your aura. People want to hear your ideas; they want to explore your mind. People want to be your friend. They want to be close to you. They want you in their life.

Even if no one has told you lately, trust me, people love you.

It is of utmost importance that you cultivate a trusting relationship with yourself.

You must practice listening to your intuition.
You must allow your gut feelings to guide you.

Your highest self will never lead you astray.

The more you get to know yourself, the more you will understand God.

And the more you get to know God, the more you will understand yourself.

You build your confidence by pursuing the things you're afraid of.

Confidence is built slowly, piece by piece, bit by bit. If you only focus on the end goal, you will always feel insecure and incapable. There are many steps in between that are crucial to your development.

You must pursue the things that scare you, you must accept the possibility of failure.

In doing this, you unlock new opportunities and become confident in your abilities.

If you really want it, you must bet on yourself first.

You must believe in yourself first; you must cultivate the confidence to go after what you want. You must intrinsically believe you are worthy of what you wish for. You must put yourself out there, even when the uncertainty is sinking inside you.

Stop waiting for recognition.

Stop waiting for someone to tell you you're good enough.

If we only pursue something after others have approved of it, our action is not rooted in our internal beliefs, but is fueled by external validation. We put our confidence into the hands of other humans.

The universe shows up for you once you show up for yourself.

Someone else's beauty does not take away from your beauty. Someone else's talent does not minimize your skills. Someone else's success does not restrict your opportunities.

There is an abundance of beauty, an abundance of talent, an abundance of opportunity.

There is more than enough space for everyone to succeed.

Staying grounded is key to increasing your capacity.

When you move through life in a chaotic manner, jumping from one thing to the next, you will eventually experience burn out. When you don't prioritize self-care and self check-ins, you limit your capacity to get things done.

If you wish to increase your energy, you must stay aligned with yourself. If you have a busy workday, wake up extra early to set your intentions. If you're overwhelmed with a profusion of tasks, stop for a moment and write a gratitude list. If you're feeling upset, angry, or frustrated, immediately stop what you're doing and breathe. Shift your focus. Count your blessings. Remind yourself that you are in control.

It is of paramount importance that you tend to your emotional wellness.

It will determine your energy levels; it will determine the way you show up in the world.

The things you lack the energy to do are the things that will give more energy.

When you feel too tired to exercise, but choose to do it anyway, you boost your energy levels. When you think you don't have enough time to clean your home, but choose to organize anyway, you increase your capacity to get things done. When you tell yourself you don't have space in your life for leisure, but choose to create space anyway, you increase your efficiency.

It's not that you don't have enough energy, time, or space—it's that you're not prioritizing the things that make you feel good, because good things don't often come easy.

You must prioritize pouring your energy into the things that give you energy back.

One of the most profound executions of self-love is honoring who you are by pursuing the things you want to do.

When we give up on our dreams, when we sacrifice our goals, when we lose sight of our passions, we betray our most authentic self. And in that, we strip others of the opportunity to be blessed by our creations.

Following through on all the things you say you want to do is unequivocally one of the greatest acts of self-love.

Find balance in everything you do.

Have an open heart while staying true to your boundaries. Be vulnerable while protecting yourself. Offer grace and forgiveness, but never at the expense of your own wellbeing. Treat others with kindness, but do not tolerate disrespect.

When we sway too heavily on one side or the other, life becomes imbalanced. We become misaligned with our truest selves.

Remember, your source comes from your center.

Romanticize your life.

Fall in love with it. Fall in love with the small things, the seemingly insignificant things. Fall in love with exercising in the morning and making dinner every night. Fall in love with every person you meet, every sight you see. Fall in love with the way birds sing and the way plants grow. Fall in love with your daily walks, with your favorite books, your best recipes. Fall in love with your errands, fall in love with your routine.

Find love in every person, find love in every single thing.

If you continually find joy in the little moments, that joy will dwell in you everywhere you go.

Quiet confidence is the most compelling.

You don't need to prove your worth, you don't need to display your accolades or boast about your accomplishments. You don't need to explain how wonderful your life is, and you don't need others to validate that.

It is counterintuitive to convince others of your confidence.

Allow your authenticity to speak for itself.

Speak life into others.

Encourage their dreams, support their ideas.
Point out their strengths, their talents, their potential.

Sometimes all it takes is one person to remind us that we
are capable.

The universe can feel your love just by the way you show up in the world.

When you love yourself, you love God. When you love others, you love God.

When you love this world, you love God. God is love, and love is God.

The more you dedicate yourself to love, the more love will unfold in your life.

Do a good job.

It doesn't matter what you're doing. Do a good job.

Whether you're helping a friend, cooking breakfast, doing chores—it doesn't matter.
Do a good job.

Fully invest yourself in the things you're tending to.

When you pour effort from your inner core, the universe rewards you with so much more.

The more we handle our gifts with care, the more gifts we will receive.

If you want more connection in your life, start with the relationships you already have. Put down your phone and listen intently. Take time out of your day to call your family and friends to check in on them. Make a conscious effort to see the good in others. Offer love to everyone you encounter.

If you want a more fruitful career, if you are seeking financial freedom, start with the job you're working right now. Commit yourself to doing your best every day, regardless of your circumstances. Put in your utmost effort, have integrity in the work you produce. Handle your finances with foresight, have gratitude for the security you have right now.

If you want a more fulfilling life, start appreciating your current one. Wake up and set your intentions for the day. Make a list of your priorities and create space for the things you love. Stand up for yourself, tend to your emotions, especially the difficult ones. Spend time pursuing your purpose. Work earnestly toward the person you want to become.

It all starts with the small things.

If you can appreciate your present moment and have gratitude for your current circumstances, you will attract your most desired future.

Even when you have the ideal relationship, the spacious home, the fruitful garden, the beautiful family—*life is still going to be life.*

You're still going to run late; you're still going to lose your keys and spill your coffee. Your lunch order is going to come out wrong and your hair is going to get cut too short. You're going to be blamed for things you can't control and you're going to be judged by people who don't know you. You're going to lose loved ones and you're going to experience seasons of setbacks.

All of life's troubles that are happening today are never going to go away. So rather than basing your happiness on what's happening, you must create it from your core.

Because no matter how big and beautiful your life is—*life is still going to be life.*

If you can't appreciate the present, you won't appreciate the future.

It's a beautiful thing to be a visionary, to want more for your life, to incessantly chase after growth and expansion. However, there are many beautiful moments in between now and the future that we must learn to fall in love with.

If we continually base our happiness on what's to come—we will never attain true joy. True joy is not contingent upon external factors. True joy does not come from material goods or extrinsic validation. True joy is cultivated from within.

This is why many people feel endlessly empty, regardless of what they achieve.

You must learn to master the gift of gratitude.
You must devote yourself to creating unconditional delight.

Everything you are looking for is within you.
Keep digging.

A scarcity mindset is not dependent on what you do or don't have.

Some people have it all but feel as though they have nothing. Others have nothing, but feel as though they have it all.

If you want to truly enjoy your life, you need to start now.

Happiness isn't something that happens to you.
It's not something on the horizon. Happiness isn't something you wait for, it's not something you gain. It's not something you have to work for or earn.

You are responsible for creating your own happiness.

You're responsible for finding the things that light you up. You're responsible for putting time aside for the things you love. You're responsible for crafting a life that contains all the things that give you joy.

I hope you learn how to love selflessly—how to give and receive love without attachment. I hope you come to see that the love you've been looking for has always been inside of you. I hope you view your worth as unwavering, completely independent from external validation. I hope you hold others to the same standard that you hold yourself. I hope you put yourself first and stop pouring your energy into the things that exhaust you. I hope you fill all the empty spaces with the things you love. I hope you take art classes and music lessons and discover all the things that make your heart beat deeper. I hope you stop making decisions based on the opinions of others and I hope you build the courage to make decisions for yourself. I hope you pursue every little thing that scares you and I hope you come to see that your fears will always lead you to fulfillment. I hope you use your growth as a means to help others, and I hope the transformation doesn't stop with you, but creates a perpetual cycle of inspiration.

I hope you allow love to lead the way.
I hope you decide the time to start is today.

The more attention you give to the things you love, the less attention you pay to the ones who don't love you.

You don't need a partner to do the things you want to do.

Go outside and enjoy life on your own.
Take full advantage of your freedom, put yourself as your highest priority.

There is such a short lapse of time that you get to only focus on yourself.

Go be with her, enjoy her, learn about her, and love her.

When we are secure in ourselves, we are free to give and receive the most authentic love.

Our love is not based on a need for validation. Our love does not come with contingencies, it is not a means to fill an empty space. Our love is not manipulated, it is not calculated, it is not conditional nor conceited.

Love is free and it should always feel that way.

Have an open heart and then let it be broken. Open it once more and let it shatter all over again.

Don't you see? The only thing holding you back is your fear of heartbreak. So what if they leave you? You will still have yourself. And what if they break your heart? You've gone through it before, you can surely get through it again.

Once you've made a home in yourself, you stop fearing love because you have accepted its potential demise. You know well enough that not all good things will last forever. You no longer allow someone's exit to erase you.

Love is both beautiful and painful.
It is miraculous and monstrous.

If you wish to experience it at its greatest capacity, you must accept its duality.

When you hold space for yourself, you create more space for love.

You free yourself to see the best in everyone. You allow yourself to feel joy, to perceive life through rose-colored lenses. You recognize beauty and feel pain, but you accept that life will inevitably have a rhythmical flow of good moments and bad moments. You offer grace and goodness; you plant seeds of inspiration everywhere that you go. You give love freely and accept hardship with gratitude.

You flow in a state of such high self-worth, just by existing, you pour love into the earth.

Life is going to work out perfectly.

All the right things are going to happen. All the right people are going to come, and all the wrong people are going to leave. You're going to have a beautiful home that brings you peace, and you're going to have a dynamic career that gives you purpose. You're going to wake up next to the love of your life and spill sweet words over morning coffee. You're going to have slow Sundays and wholesome holidays. Your art is going to be impactful and you're going to be recognized for your devotion. You're going to travel and see the world and you're going to encounter incredible people along the way. You're going to be seen for who you are and appreciated for all that you do.

Don't worry so much my friend, life is going to work out perfectly.

Your season of singleness is crucial to your development.

One day you will have the relationship, the family, all the love and connection you've always dreamed of. You will be surrounded by people to pour your love into, and they will give you their love right back.

But right now, the only person asking for your attention is yourself. You are the only one in need of your affection.

By loving yourself now, you prepare yourself for great love in the future.

Everything you desire is moving towards you.

There is no rush, there is no need for questions or concerns.
Don't worry so much about the details.
Don't worry so much about when and where or why
and how.

God planted your desires for a divine reason. But before
the seeds can sprout, you must build a fruitful founda-
tion. You must grow your gratitude; you must water your
self-worth.

Rest in confidence that this universe will always take care
of you.

You deserve a consistent love.

You deserve a love that chooses you every day. You deserve a love that is sure, a love that is steady, a love that is soft in all its forms. You deserve a love that sees you at your best and meets you at your worst.

You deserve a peaceful love, a playful love, a love that prioritizes you through every season of life.

When you let go of attachment, you free yourself to fully enjoy life.

You are liberated in your love; you fully relish in moments of connection without fixating on the future. You allow yourself to enjoy experiences without the aching anxiety about when it's going to end.

You know that regardless of what happens, regardless of who leaves your life—you will still have yourself, and that will always be enough.

So anything else, any lovely person, any once-in-a-lifetime experience, is simply an added benefit to the beautiful life you've already created within yourself.

Be with someone who makes you feel safe.

Someone who makes you feel seen and secure. Be with someone who reminds you how beautiful life is and how wonderful it is to share your experiences together. Be with someone who challenges you, someone who helps you grow from your mistakes, someone who helps you fall in love with your flaws. Be with someone who is your greatest defender, your best friend, the person who will stand by you through all your endeavors.

Be with someone who is dedicated to loving you and lifting you up.

The more aligned you are with yourself, the more you attract what is meant for you.

When you show up as your most authentic self, you gravitate toward people who love you for who you truly are. When you honor your core values, you call in opportunities that exceed your expectations.

When you pursue your deepest desires, you tap into the power of the divine.

You will always receive what you authentically desire.

Your deepest desires derive from the divine. There is meaning behind the voice calling you towards something greater. There is purpose in the presence pushing you in a different direction. There is a reason you feel what you feel, there is a reason you want what you want.

You were born with particular passions, certain skills, and intuitive instincts for a reason. One day everything you desire will come to fruition because it was destined by the divine. But for that to happen, you must first honor what you feel. You must go after what you want.

Don't worry so much about if you can do it or how you will achieve it. Listen to the whispers inside of you. Put trust in your inner knowing. Take one small step in the right direction every day.

You will eventually find yourself at the finish line, realizing there was indeed a reason behind everything.

You're being watched over even when you don't know it.
You're being guided even when you can't feel it.
You're being protected even when you can't see it.

Everything in your life is piecing together perfectly, elegantly orchestrated by the most powerful force in this world.

Your impact is perpetual.

When you live a purposeful life, your influence is everlasting. Your legacy does not end with you. The people you inspire will one day inspire others, and those people will become inspirations too. When you live a purposeful life, you create a cycle of stimulation, a rhythm of revelation.

Your energy will echo through every generation.

One of the most beautiful things about this world is that it will *always* lead you back to yourself.

Regardless of how hard you try to veer off course—you will *always* be led back to your truth.

The universe will never stop fighting for you to find your destiny.

I hope you soak in your solitude. I hope you learn to celebrate your singleness. I hope you selfishly use every lasting second of your life to discover all the things that make your heart beat deeper. I hope you go on long walks and look at birds and trees and I hope you fantasize about all your future dreams. I hope you meet people that make you smile and teach you new things. I hope you lay in parks and listen to people laugh, and children play, and I hope you feel inspired by the constant chatter of life. I hope you connect deeper with yourself and finally express the creativity that's been boiling inside you. I hope you find more love, and I hope you fall out of love, and let go of love, and laugh and cry at every inconvenience in between.

I hope you learn to live life on your own terms.
I hope you awaken your most authentic self.
I hope you discover all the things that excite you.

I hope you finally come home to yourself.

DÉJÀ RAE is a New York City-based writer originally from California. Since she was young, her inquisitive mind has led her on a perpetual journey towards enlightenment and self-discovery. Both introspective and analytical, Déjà Rae's work focuses on identifying patterns in the world and articulating shared human emotions. With a bachelor's degree in psychology and a master's degree in international development, Déjà Rae hopes to use her education and creative skills to empower others to chase after their most authentic selves.

instagram.com/ebbandflowpoetry

MORE FROM

THOUGHT CATALOG BOOKS

A Gentle Reminder
—*Bianca Sparacino*

Ceremony
—*Brianna Wiest*

Everything You'll Ever Need
(You Can Find Within Yourself)
—*Charlotte Freeman*

All That You Deserve
—*Jaqueline Whitney*

**THOUGHT
CATALOG**
Books

THOUGHTCATALOG.COM
NEW YORK · LOS ANGELES